SPORTS HEROES AND LEGENDS

Lance Armstrong

Read all of the books in this exciting, action-packed biography series!

Hank Aaron
Muhammad Ali
Lance Armstrong
Barry Bonds
Roberto Clemente
Joe DiMaggio
Tim Duncan
Dale Earnhardt Jr.
Lou Gehrig
Mia Hamm
Tony Hawk
Derek Jeter
Michael Jordan
Sandy Koufax
Michelle Kwan
Mickey Mantle
Shaquille O'Neal
Jesse Owens
Jackie Robinson
Alex Rodriguez
Wilma Rudolph
Babe Ruth
Ichiro Suzuki
Tiger Woods

SPORTS HEROES AND LEGENDS

Lance Armstrong

by Matt Doeden

BARNES & NOBLE
NEW YORK

For Mom

This 2006 edition published by Barnes & Noble Publishing, Inc. by arrangement with Lerner Publications Company, a division of Lerner Publishing Group, Minneapolis, MN.

Cover photograph:
© Elizabeth Kreutz/NewSport/Corbis

Sports Heroes and Legends™ is a trademark of Barnes & Noble Publishing, Inc.

2006 Barnes & Noble Publishing

ISBN-13: 978-0-7607-7517-2
ISBN-10: 0-7607-7517-6

Printed and bound in the United States of America

1 3 5 7 9 10 8 6 4 2

Contents

Prologue

Comeback Kid

As Lance Armstrong climbed on his bike the morning of July 17, 2001, he looked up at the mountain peaks of the Pyrenees in southern France. The twenty-nine-year-old American cancer survivor had won the Tour de France, cycling's greatest race, twice in a row. The grueling race covered more than 3,200 kilometers (1,988 miles) over three weeks. If Lance was going to make it three wins in a row, he had a lot of work to do. Entering stage 10 of a twenty-stage race, Lance was in twenty-third place, more than 35 minutes behind the leader. No Tour cyclist had ever come back to win from so far behind.

Still, Lance and his teammates on the U.S. Postal Service team were confident. The first nine stages of the race had been on mostly flat ground. But the Tour was entering the mountains. Stage 10, an agonizing 209-kilometer (130-mile) climb through the Pyrenees, was exactly the kind of ride Lance could dominate.

Many of the riders ahead of him were sprinters—excellent riders on flat ground. But most of them would struggle with the difficult climb of more than 6,000 feet over three mountain peaks.

One of Lance's biggest challengers for the title was Germany's Jan Ullrich. Early in the stage, Lance and his teammates let Ullrich lead the way. They wanted him out in front doing the hardest work. In cycling, riding behind someone is easier than leading because the rear cyclist meets less air resistance—a strategy called drafting. The stage would take more than six hours, and Lance didn't want to wear out his legs too early. Better to let the competition do all the work.

As he rode, Lance used a radio headset to talk to the team coach, Johan Bruyneel. Together, they formed a plan. Lance would pretend to be struggling in the ride. He would look tired and beaten. Because he was a two-time champion, he knew the television cameras would be on him. If he looked worn out, Ullrich and the others might attack and push themselves too hard. Lance could ride at the back of the peloton (pack of riders), while his rivals did even more work.

Lance did his best acting job. He hung his head. He sent his teammates to bring him extra water bottles. The act fooled everybody. TV broadcasters quickly noticed that the race's defending champion was lagging behind. "It's a long way back to see Armstrong," one announcer said. "He does not look good, and he should not be riding so far down the group; he's obviously having a horrendous day."

At the front of the peloton, Ullrich was among those who fell for the bluff. The leaders attacked hard, standing and pumping the pedals as fast as they could. They wanted to set a pace so fast that Lance would drop, or fall away from the group. If they had a chance to end his hopes of winning a third straight Tour, they were going to take it.

Still, Lance stayed in the back, waiting. He was more than 7 minutes behind Ullrich and the stage leader, Laurent Roux. But that was okay. It was all according to his plan.

Finally, at the foot of a mountain called the Alpe d'Huez, the time came to attack. Lance nodded to his teammates and stomped down on the pedals. They sailed through the peloton, eating up huge chunks of the lead Ullrich and Roux had built. As the road started to ascend into the stage's final climb, Lance sailed around a sharp turn. There, in front of him, was Ullrich. The German was struggling with the climb, exhausted from a day of leading and from his early attack. Lance's bluff had worked—he had fooled his rival into using up his strength too early.

"Armstrong has maybe been playing an incredible poker game today by sitting at the back and letting everybody else do the work," said a TV broadcaster.

As Lance sped by Ullrich, he looked back over his shoulder. He wanted to see the expression on the German's face—wanted to know whether Ullrich was truly beaten. He got his answer quickly. Lance surged forward again to see if his rival could keep up. He couldn't. Soon, Lance passed Roux as well and sailed to the finish line, almost a full 2 minutes ahead of Ullrich. He shook his arms in the air and hopped off the bike.

Lance was back in the race. But in the overall standings, he still trailed France's François Simon by 20 minutes. He hoped his furious attack hadn't left him too tired for the next day. Stage 11 was another tough climb, this time a 32-kilometer (20-mile) time trial. A time trial stage is different from a regular stage. Riders don't all leave the starting line at the same time. They start spaced 3 minutes apart. They cannot rely on their teammates and drafting. They have to do the work on their own.

Again, Lance was measuring himself against Jan Ullrich, who started before him. As Lance crossed each checkpoint (spots for tracking progress), his coach told him his times. He was faster than Ullrich—a lot faster. With about 4 kilometers (2.5 miles) to go, he was ahead of the German by 42 seconds. He pushed hard toward the finish line and crossed with a time of 1 hour, 7 minutes, 27 seconds, a full minute faster than Ullrich, who finished second. The climb pulled Lance to within 13 minutes of the lead, still held by Simon.

Lance kept up the fierce pace. He cut the lead to 9:10 in stage 12, then made his big move during the 194-kilometer (120.5-mile) stage 13. He and Ullrich both rode at the front for most of the stage. Before the last of six climbs, Lance attacked hard. Ullrich couldn't keep up. Again, the German had to watch Lance pull away and win another mountain stage. Lance blew away the whole field and took over the yellow jersey, the cycling shirt worn by the leader of the Tour de France. In only four stages of racing, Lance had made the biggest comeback in Tour history—he'd gone from 35 minutes behind to more than 3 minutes ahead.

He seemed unstoppable. Ullrich, badly beaten again, was discouraged. "I tried everything that was possible," he said. "I have to wait for a black day for Armstrong, otherwise he is unbeatable."

Ullrich feared what most of the other riders knew. With a 3-minute lead, only a disaster would stop Lance Armstrong. No disaster came. Lance won one more stage, the eighteenth, and cruised into Paris for the final stage with a 6-minute win over second-place Ullrich. After more than eighty-six hours on the bike, Lance was the champion—for the third year in a row.

"It's the best feeling," Lance said. "As always, I am happy to finally arrive, to finally finish the Tour. It's a special feeling."

Chapter One

Humble Beginnings

Lance Armstrong started his life as the baby only one person wanted. His father didn't really want a baby. His mother's mother didn't want her teenage daughter to have a baby. The only person who truly wanted the healthy baby boy was his mother, Linda Gayle Mooneyham.

Linda was just a high school student in Dallas, Texas, when she found out she was pregnant with Lance. At first, she tried to hide her pregnancy with baggy clothing. But soon, it was impossible to hide. Many of her friends and family tried to convince her to give up the baby for adoption. She was too young, they thought, to be raising a child.

But Linda had different ideas. She was going to start a family, and the first step was marrying the baby's father, Eddie Gunderson. Marriage wasn't what Gunderson wanted, but he went along with the plan. The couple lived in a small apartment.

Linda's mom, who still didn't support her daughter's decision, almost never came to help. Linda and Eddie took part-time jobs and did what they could to make ends meet. They even worked together on a paper route.

When Linda was pregnant with Lance, she was convinced that the baby would be a girl. She had even picked out a name—Erica.

On September 18, 1971, Linda gave birth to a 9-pound, 12-ounce baby boy. She was thrilled. She named the boy Lance after her favorite football player, a wide receiver for the Dallas Cowboys named Lance Rentzel. The childbirth was difficult for Linda, though. She developed a high fever after giving birth. Nurses took care of the baby while she recovered. Almost two days passed before she was able to hold and spend time with little Lance.

Things didn't get any easier when she got the baby back home. Eddie wasn't ready for the responsibility of fatherhood. In his frustration, he sometimes lashed out at Linda. He often left her alone with the baby. For support, Linda turned to her father, Paul Mooneyham, who was divorced from her mother.

Eventually, Linda left Eddie and moved in with her father full-time. Eddie begged her to come back, but Linda knew their relationship was over.

Life with her father was better for Linda and Lance. Father and daughter worked together to care for the baby. Linda watched the baby at night while Paul worked. Paul watched Lance during the day while Linda searched for a job.

Soon, Linda and Lance moved out. They got a small apartment in Oak Cliff, Texas, near Dallas. While she finished high school, Linda worked part-time at a Kentucky Fried Chicken on the corner. She also worked at a small grocery store. She later found a job at the local post office. The jobs didn't pay much, but the little family got by. "All I did, my life, was going to work and raising my son, and I was happy to do it," Linda said.

Trying to earn enough money and still care for Lance was hard on Linda, but she remembers plenty of good times. She loved to read to little Lance. They danced together. She took him on walks, and they went swimming. Lance was in a hurry to keep up with his mother. He started walking when he was only nine months old.

Lance was just a toddler when he had his first fall on a bicycle. Linda and Eddie had divorced, but Eddie still got to visit his son. Once, Eddie wanted to take Lance for a bike ride. As Eddie pedaled, he thought Lance was holding on tight behind him. But the little boy took a nasty fall off the bike. Eddie had to rush him to the hospital for stitches. Linda was furious. She believed that Eddie had proven he couldn't be a good father. Linda told him he couldn't visit Lance anymore.

Lance's first vehicle was a small three-wheeler called a Green Machine. He got it for his second birthday and rode it constantly.

When Lance was three, Linda found a job as a secretary and moved to Richardson, Texas, a suburb of Dallas. She also had a new man in her life, a salesman named Terry Armstrong, whom she married. In time, Terry adopted Lance as his own son, and Lance took on Terry's last name.

Armstrong tried to be a good father to Lance, but he was often misguided. He used a paddle to punish the boy, even for small misbehaviors. He also treated Linda poorly. But he helped pay for everything the family needed, and financial security was important to Linda. She no longer had to worry about having enough money to provide for Lance.

Across the street from Lance's home in Richardson was a store called the Richardson Bike Mart. Jim Hoyt, the owner of the store, often saw Linda and Lance together. He admired how hard Linda worked to raise her son and thought Lance was a fine young boy. When Lance was seven, Hoyt gave Linda a great deal on Lance's first bike. It was a brown Schwinn Mag Scrambler, a BMX model with yellow wheels. Lance loved the bike. To him, the bike represented a freedom he'd never had before. He rode it whenever he could.

Terry Armstrong coached Lance's Little League baseball team. But although Lance enjoyed the sport, he wasn't a natural star.

When Lance was twelve, the family moved to a new house in Plano, Texas, north of Dallas. Lance was growing up to be a strong boy. He spent hours playing baseball and football. Football is a favorite sport in Texas. It's how young men make a name for themselves, and Lance was eager to prove himself. Despite his strength and athletic ability, Lance had no real talent for football and quickly gave up on the sport.

But he didn't give up on being an athlete. He wanted to compete—and win. Lance learned about a distance-running race held by his school. He had no formal experience in distance running, but he insisted on entering the race. He told his mother he was going to win. He came through on the promise, one of his first tastes of victory in a race. The win was especially sweet because Lance beat many boys who were star football players. He proved to himself that he was a good athlete too.

Some of Lance's friends had joined a community swimming club, and he wanted to try swimming as well. At first, his attempts to swim looked like a disaster. He flopped into the water with no idea what to do. Although he was twelve years old, he had to take swimming classes with kids almost half his age. But as bad as he was at first, he worked hard to improve.

> "*He seemed to have a core of pure energy that threw off sparks when it wasn't being channeled in the right direction. He was . . . exhaustingly creative when it came to manufacturing fun and mischief.*"
>
> —LANCE'S MOTHER

Chris MacCurdy, a coach at the swimming club, saw that Lance worked hard and had a lot of stamina. MacCurdy worked with Lance on his technique. Something must have clicked, because this help quickly turned Lance into one of the club's best swimmers. By age thirteen, he was one of the top swimmers in Texas in his age group. He swam in the 1,500-meter freestyle, a race in which swimmers are free to use any swimming stroke they wish.

A problem soon developed with Lance's newest passion. The swimming club was about 10 miles from his home, but often his mother was busy working and couldn't drive him to practice. He wasn't about to let this stop him, though. He would climb on his bike and ride the 10 miles to the club, swim for several hours, then ride home again. It was a grueling schedule, but Lance didn't complain. If that was what he had to do to compete, then that was what he'd do.

Chapter Two

Junior

By age thirteen, Lance had proven himself to be a good runner and an excellent swimmer. He was always on his bike, pedaling away. So when he saw an advertisement for a junior triathlon called IronKids, it seemed like a perfect fit.

A triathlon is a race with three parts. Competitors begin the race with a swim, then climb onto bikes for a long ride. At the end of the ride, the racers jump off their bikes and begin a distance run. Triathlon is an exhausting sport for which few people are suited. But it was perfect for Lance. Excited, he told his mother about the race. Linda, who was beginning to think Lance might have a future as an athlete, shared his enthusiasm. The two went out and bought a multispeed racing bike called a Mercier for the race.

Lance hadn't ever raced in or even seen a triathlon before. He hadn't done any special training for the race. But that didn't slow him down. He started off strong in the swimming part and was one of the first racers out of the water. In the second part, the cycling, he pulled out to a big lead. When he finished that part of the race, he jumped off the bike and put on running shoes. He took off toward the finish line with nobody else in sight. He easily won the race, blowing away all his competition. A few weeks later, he won a second junior triathlon in Houston, Texas.

Lance was hooked. The triathlon combined three of his favorite sports. It required great endurance and determination, and he had both. Unlike many competitors, Lance didn't mind the pain in his muscles during a race. He would later write, "If it was a suffer-fest, I was good at it."

Teenage Lance dreamed of one day competing in the Olympics. His mom once gave him a key chain that said "1988"—the year of the next Summer Olympics.

While Lance was proving himself to be one of the state's top young athletes, his home life wasn't happy. His stepfather was becoming a bigger problem. Terry Armstrong didn't treat Linda with respect. He punished Lance too severely. Lance once ran away from home after a fight with Terry and didn't come back until the next day. Soon, Linda left her husband. Once again, Lance was all she had, and she was all he had. But he was old enough to help his mother. He did chores around the house. He was also earning his own money by winning triathlons.

Even though he was just fifteen, Lance wanted to test his skills against the best adults. He entered the 1987 President's Triathlon in Lake Lavon, Texas. Nobody expected a teenage kid to keep up with the large field of experienced adult athletes. But he held his own, finishing thirty-second.

He entered more adult triathlons and started winning some of them. Soon, his name was becoming known. The adults called him Junior and marveled at how a boy could beat so many grown men. *Triathlete* magazine named him the national Rookie of the Year in sprint triathlons (short triathlons). The magazine said he was one of the greatest athletes the sport had ever seen. He was a rising star. And he was making good prize money—about $20,000 a year—by age sixteen.

The biking segments of the triathlon quickly became Lance's strength. He worked hard on his cycling and started entering bike races called criteriums, or crits. These popular races featured some of the best riders in Texas. Lance joined a racing team sponsored by Jim Hoyt (the bicycle shop owner who had helped Lance get his first bike) and the Richardson Bike Mart. Lance quickly moved up from crits for beginners to races for the most skilled riders. He also continued to compete in triathlons.

Jim Hoyt

Jim Hoyt was one of the father figures in Lance's life. He'd been a cyclist before fighting in the Vietnam War at age nineteen. When he got back from Vietnam, he opened a bike store and did his best to help young riders, including Lance.

By this time, Lance was attending classes at Plano East High School. School was never his main priority, though. He was always on his bike, pedaling mile after mile. He would ride all the way into Dallas. He was strong and confident—sometimes too confident. He would ride in Dallas's heavy traffic, dodging cars and running through stoplights. One time, his overconfidence got him into serious trouble. He ran through a stoplight and got hit by a truck. The impact threw Lance from the bike onto the street. He wasn't wearing a helmet. He smashed his head against the street and got a big gash on his foot. An ambulance took him to the hospital. His bike was ruined.

Lance's doctors put some stitches in his head and his foot and told him he wouldn't be able to race for a while. But Lance didn't want to hear that. His next triathlon was less than a week away. He borrowed a friend's bike and entered the race anyway, despite the painful wound on his foot. Lance's doctor was later shocked to learn that his young patient had ignored the pain and finished third in the event.

As a teenager, Lance loved to listen to heavy metal music, especially the band Metallica.

As Lance continued to train, he felt more and more comfortable on the bike. Soon, dreams of being a professional road racer replaced his dreams of being a star in the triathlon.

In September 1989, during his last year of high school, Lance entered a 12-mile time trial in Moriarty, New Mexico. Because each rider starts separately in a time trial, Lance would be competing only against the clock. The course was flat and easy to ride, which meant that many riders could score their best times. Lance knew a good time would impress people in the cycling world. He needed to be in top form.

But when Lance arrived at the time trial, he realized he'd made a mistake. He hadn't planned on cold weather. He had only his normal cycling clothes. As he prepared for the race in the chilly morning air, he couldn't get warmed up. He knew he wouldn't do well in the time trial if he started out cold. He ran to find his mom. Linda had only a small pink jacket. Lance was far too big for the jacket, but he put it on anyway. He turned up the heat in his mom's car and tried his best to stay warm. When it was finally time to start, Lance climbed out of the car and onto the bike. Despite his earlier fears, Lance was on top of his game. He didn't just do well in the time trial—he broke the course record by an amazing 45 seconds.

Lance's cycling career was off to a great start. The U.S. Cycling Federation, a national association for bicycle racers, had learned about his performance at Moriarty. Federation officials asked Lance to join the U.S. junior cycling team and go to Moscow, Russia, for the 1990 Junior World Championships. The chance to join the team and compete overseas was huge. Lance excitedly told administrators at his school that he needed to be excused from classes to take part. But the school officials weren't impressed. They told Lance he didn't have permission to miss class.

Lance went anyway. He started by training with the team in Colorado. Then he flew to Moscow for the race, a time trial.

Lance started with a bang. His first few laps around the course were the fastest in the field. But he tired out by the end and had a disappointing finish. Even so, the newcomer had impressed many cycling experts. They thought that with the proper coaching, Lance had the tools to become a very exciting cyclist.

> For his senior prom, Lance rented a limousine. As he was getting ready to leave and pick up his date, he told his mom to put on a dress and join him. He knew she'd never been in a limo, and he wanted her to share in the fun. Linda rode around with Lance and his date until it was time for the couple to go to the dance.

Lance came home feeling good about himself, but those good feelings quickly disappeared. He learned that because he had left school without permission, he wouldn't be able to graduate. Linda found a small private school called Bending Oaks that would allow Lance to graduate if he finished a few courses. He didn't graduate with his old classmates, but Lance still got his diploma. He was ready to leave home and start a full-time career as a cyclist.

Chapter Three

Growing Pains

In 1990 Lance moved out on his own. He settled in Austin, Texas, where he rented an apartment. He also joined the U.S. national cycling team under coach Chris Carmichael. Carmichael saw that the eighteen-year-old Texan was a powerful rider with enormous potential. But he also saw a young man who was stubborn and hadn't had much coaching. Lance wanted to ride at full blast all the time. He didn't understand the strategy of holding a little energy in reserve.

Lance's first race for the team was the 1990 Amateur World Championship in Japan. The race, held on a very hot day, was 115 miles long, with a difficult uphill section. Carmichael wanted Lance to draft—to stay behind other riders and save some energy for the end of the race.

But Lance didn't listen to his coach. He was overconfident and quickly pedaled to a big lead. The lead grew and grew to almost 90 seconds, but Lance was exhausting himself. He got tired and slowed down. His lead fell to a minute, then to 30 seconds. Soon the peloton had caught him. Lance couldn't mount a charge at the end. He could only slide back into the draft and finish eleventh. It was a disappointing finish after the fast start. But despite the mistake, Lance's time was the fastest by an American rider in more than fifteen years.

Greg LeMond

Greg LeMond was the first truly famous American cyclist. In 1986 LeMond became the first non-European to win the Tour de France. But then disaster struck—he was accidentally shot in the chest while hunting. LeMond made a remarkable recovery and came back to win two more Tours, in 1989 and 1990.

Impatience wasn't Lance's only problem during races. His aggressive style also got him into trouble. He didn't give his opponents any respect. He would shout at them and insult them during races. He wouldn't work with his own teammates. He would show them up, just to prove that he was better. In response, other riders sometimes got in his way on purpose and tried to slow him down. They refused to draft with him. By being selfish, Lance was isolating himself.

Lance didn't like the idea, common in team racing, that one racer should move over to let another one win. This situation came into focus in a race in Italy shortly after the 1990 Amateur Worlds. Lance was riding as an amateur on the U.S. cycling team (amateur cyclists get paid, but they can't win prize money at international events). He had also signed on with a professional team called Subaru-Montgomery. Both teams were competing in the race.

Professional cycling teams are often a mix of riders from different countries. For instance, Lance's Motorola team, sponsored by a U.S. company, had many European riders.

The race was held over ten stages, each on a different day. As the race went on, only one rider, an American named Nate Reese, was ahead of Lance. One evening between stages, Eddie Borysewicz, the coach of the Subaru-Montgomery team, told Lance that he was expected to help Reese, a professional, win the race.

Lance didn't know what to do. He wasn't used to the idea of staying back to let somebody else win. He talked to Coach Carmichael about it. His coach told him to ignore Borysewicz. If Lance had a chance to win, Carmichael said, he had to take it. Lance also phoned Linda back in Texas. She agreed with Carmichael. Lance had to ride the best he could.

Lance followed Carmichael's advice. In the next stage, he pushed hard to take over the lead. His fast pace left Reese far behind. This decision made Lance very unpopular with the professionals on the Subaru-Montgomery team, and he knew it would cost him his spot on the team. In addition, the Italian fans were angry that an American was leading the race. They threw glass and tacks onto the road, hoping to make Lance blow a tire.

It didn't matter, though. Lance crossed the finish line first, with a margin of victory of more than a minute. It was a rare American win in a European cycling event. The twenty-year-old amateur had finally made his mark on the cycling world. That night, Carmichael told Lance something he would never forget. The coach said, "You're gonna win the Tour de France one day."

As Lance expected, Subaru-Montgomery kicked him off the team for disobeying orders. But Lance knew that if he kept winning races, he'd have his pick of teams.

Lance was building a reputation as a strong cyclist. He won the U.S. National Amateur Championship. He trained hard for the 1992 Olympics in Barcelona, Spain. He had looked forward to the 194-kilometer (120.5-mile) Olympic road race for years. At the time, only amateur cyclists were allowed to compete in the Olympics. Lance had remained an amateur just so he could race in the Olympics.

Lance gained strength as he approached the Olympics. He won three stages at a race in Spain. He won two more time trials back in the United States. And when the time came to qualify for the U.S. Olympic cycling team, he finished a solid second.

Eddy Merckx

One of Lance's cycling heroes is Eddy Merckx. The legendary Belgian cyclist won more bike races than anyone during the 1960s and 1970s. He is also a five-time winner of the Tour de France.

Chris Carmichael, who coached the Olympic team, tried to work out a winning strategy for Lance. He told one of Lance's teammates to make an early charge in the race. Carmichael hoped that all the other leading cyclists would go with the early charger. At the same time, Lance would stay behind and wait until the end to make an attack.

Early in the race, the plan seemed to be working perfectly. But when the time came for Lance to charge, he didn't have the energy. He pedaled as hard as he could, but he just couldn't catch up to the lead pack. He finished a disappointing fourteenth. Not only had he failed to win the gold medal (won by his friend Fabio Casartelli of Italy), he hadn't even been close to medaling.

With the Olympics past him, Lance knew it was time to finally turn professional. He was already making a living at cycling, but going pro would allow him to collect prize money in international events. Coach Jim Ochowicz, nicknamed Och, signed Lance to ride for a cycling team sponsored by Motorola, a company that makes phones and other communications devices. Ochowicz was an old friend of Chris Carmichael, so he was already familiar with what Lance could do on a bike. "I want to go to Europe and be a pro," Lance told Ochowicz. "I don't want to just be good at it, I want to be the best."

With his new contract and new team, Lance packed his bags and moved to Italy. He and his teammates stayed in hotels during races. Eventually, Lance rented an apartment in Lake Como, Italy. The apartment served as his home base in Europe. He even learned to speak a little Spanish, Italian, French, and Dutch.

His first race as a pro was the 1992 Clásica San Sebastián in northern Spain. This one-day race is one of ten in cycling's

World Cup series. As the race got under way, Lance was battered by cold winds and heavy rains, conditions he wasn't used to from his days in Texas. Soaking wet, Lance couldn't keep pace with the peloton. He wasn't the only one struggling, though. Several other riders simply quit the race. From the back of the pack, Lance thought about joining them. But quitting wasn't Lance's style. Instead, he fought through the pain and the cold and crossed the finish line. The crowd hooted and made fun of Lance as he crossed, last of 111 finishers.

It was a terrible start to Lance's professional career. After a disappointing Olympics and an embarrassing first professional race, his confidence was as low as it had ever been. Lance thought about quitting the sport. Maybe it wasn't right for him. Maybe the competition at the professional level was just too tough. He called Chris Carmichael and told him about the disaster. His friend talked him out of quitting. Carmichael told Lance to learn from his failure and become a better cyclist because of it. Reluctantly, Lance agreed. He would keep trying.

Lance didn't have much time to feel sorry for himself. Two days later, he was riding in the Championship of Zurich in Switzerland. He had a lot at stake in the race—his reputation, his pride, and, most important, his confidence in himself.

He started the race the best way he knew how—by attacking. He would leave strategy for another day. On this day, Lance was going all out. He powered himself to the front of the peloton. As the race wore on, more and more cyclists fell back, unable to keep up with the blistering pace. But not Lance. While he didn't win the race, his second-place finish proved that he belonged in the professional ranks. The finish was a much-needed boost to the young cyclist's confidence.

Random Drug Control

As a professional cyclist, Lance had to take random drug tests. Cycling agents could show up at his door anytime, any day, and ask for a urine sample. If Lance, or any cyclist, refused to take the test, he would be considered guilty of doping—or taking performance-enhancing drugs.

Not long after his strong finish, Lance entered the Tour of the Mediterranean in Italy. He started the race out front and soon found himself riding alongside Italian cycling legend Moreno Argentin. When Argentin mistook Lance for another rider, the young American grew angry. He was insulted that the Italian didn't know his name. Lance taunted and cursed at Argentin. He attacked and attacked until he ran out of energy. He'd ridden too hard.

The bad feelings between the two riders carried over into the next race, a one-day event in Italy called the Trophée Laigueglia. Again, Lance targeted Argentin. Again, he attacked. But since this was a shorter race, Lance didn't tire. As they sprinted toward the finish line, the four leaders pedaled with everything they had. With determination, Lance powered to the lead and crossed the finish line first. But behind him, something unusual happened. Argentin slammed on his brakes. He let the other two riders cross the finish line before him.

At first, this action confused Lance. But quickly, he understood the veteran cyclist's message. Argentin had finished fourth on purpose. The top three finishers stand together on the podium to receive medals. Argentin preferred finishing fourth to standing next to Lance. It was the biggest insult he could give the young American. It was also a lesson that Lance took to heart. He realized that he needed to stop making enemies.

As summer approached, Lance was getting more attention, both for his success and for his racing style. Many cyclists enjoy the attention that success brings. But Lance wasn't ready for it. "I don't want to be the big star," he said. "I don't want to be bothered. I want to be left alone really and allowed to race."

Chapter Four

Rising Star

The summer of 1993 was a big time in Lance's career. The exciting news in the American cycling world was a $1 million bonus being offered to any rider who could win the Triple Crown of Cycling, which was composed of three of the biggest races in the United States. The Thrift drug company offered the bonus as a way to get publicity.

Because the three races are very different, it seemed unlikely that one rider could win them all. He would have to be an expert sprinter, stage racer, and climber. The executives at Thrift never expected to have to pay the bonus.

A typical racing bike weighs about 14 pounds. Each bike has twenty gear settings.

Lance disagreed. He was making a good salary. But $1 million was a whole lot of money. It would make life comfortable for him and his mother, who had worked so hard to help him succeed.

The chase for the Triple Crown began in Pittsburgh, Pennsylvania, with the Thrift Drug Classic, a one-day sprint. Lance won the event. Next, he went to West Virginia for the West Virginia Mountain Classic. There, his powerful climbing drove him to victory in the six-day stage race. He was two-thirds of the way to his goal. All that remained was the U.S. Pro Championships in Philadelphia, Pennsylvania.

Lance was one of 120 riders who lined up to start the grueling, 156-mile lap race. The media was everywhere. In a nation where cycling isn't a big sport, Lance's quest for the Triple Crown had captured the public's attention. An estimated five hundred thousand people lined the streets of Philadelphia to watch the race.

Early on, Lance hung back, determined to ride a smart race. He wouldn't attack too soon and wear himself out. He rode along with the pack for the first 130 miles. Then, as the peloton approached one of the steepest climbs of the course, Lance decided it was time to go. He later described himself as being in a rage. He screamed as he pedaled, blowing past his competition and opening up a huge lead.

As he crossed the finish line, reporters rushed to speak to him. Lance hadn't just won the Triple Crown. He'd also won the U.S. Pro Championships by the largest margin in the history of the race. The crowd roared as Lance gave his mom a big hug. Later, as he stood on the podium to accept his trophy, Lance broke down in tears of joy.

Lactic Acid

Doctors once tested Lance's muscles to see how much lactic acid they made. Overworked muscles release lactic acid. The chemical causes muscles to ache. The doctors were amazed to find how little lactic acid Lance's muscles produce—less than 25 percent of what an average muscle does. This fact may explain why Lance is so good at fighting through pain—his muscles simply don't hurt as much as his opponents' muscles do.

Lance was looking forward to entering the 1993 Tour de France. The race, which winds throughout France and sometimes into neighboring countries, is the most famous and most grueling cycling race of them all. But first, Lance prepared for the Tour DuPont, a miniature American version of the Tour de France. Lance was hot and entered the race as one of the cyclists to beat. Right away, he proved that he would be a force, finishing second in the opening time trial.

Throughout the race, Lance battled Mexico's Raul Alcala for the lead. They raced through Delaware, Virginia, and North Carolina. They climbed the slopes of the Appalachian Mountains, side by side. Neither man could build much of a lead on the other. Finally, entering the last stage, Lance trailed Alcala by 19 seconds.

Lance had 36.5 miles to make up that 19 seconds. The final stage was a time trial, so the riders wouldn't start alongside one another. Since Alcala was the race leader, he started last. Lance started a few minutes before him.

Lance knew he was in trouble when Alcala began to catch him. When the Mexican cyclist passed him, all hope of winning seemed lost. Then Alcala's bike had a flat tire. Lance sailed past the leader, hopeful that he could earn back all the time he had lost. But Alcala's team quickly helped him change the tire and got him back on the course. The Mexican crossed the finish line with a 46-second lead.

Next up for Lance was the Tour de France. Despite his success in the United States, nobody expected him to be a factor in the race. At twenty-one, he was young and still a newcomer. And he was an American competing in an event dominated by more-experienced Europeans.

Lance wanted to make his mark. He targeted the race's eighth stage, a 184-kilometer (114-mile) ride from Châlons-sur-Marne to Verdun, France. He wasn't ready to win the whole race, but Lance could win a single stage, still a huge accomplishment. He started off the stage riding and drafting with the peloton. With about 10 kilometers (6 miles) to go, Lance and a small group of riders broke away from the pack. The sprint was on.

> Because the Tour de France is a European race, tour organizers use the metric system for measuring distances. They measure stages in kilometers, not miles.

As the finish line approached, Lance made a move to pass to the right, but Irish cyclist Stephen Roche moved over to block him. With only 100 meters (330 feet) to go, Lance let out a scream so loud that it surprised Roche, breaking his concentration for a moment. That break was all the young American needed. He powered past the leader, almost running into a roadside barrier as he did, and crossed the finish line first. Lance had achieved his goal by winning a stage at the Tour de France—becoming one of the youngest riders ever to do so.

As high as Lance was from his win, the good feelings didn't last long. Only four stages later, he dropped out of the race. After a cold, brutal climb through the Alps, he knew he could go no farther. He told reporters that the mountains were just "too long and too cold."

Climb Rankings

The Tour de France ranks climbs by category. Here are the five rankings:

- Category 4: A short, easy climb, usually less than a few miles and not too steep
- Category 3: A climb of about 5 kilometers (3 miles) at a grade, or slope, of about 5 percent
- Category 2: A climb of 5 kilometers (3 miles) or longer at a steeper grade, up to about 8 percent
- Category 1: A long climb of up to 20 kilometers (12 miles) at a grade of 5 to 6 percent
- Hors (Beyond) Category (HC): A climb so long or steep that it doesn't fit into any of the other categories

Lance's problems continued in his very next race, the Championship of Zurich. It was a typical failure—he attacked too soon and didn't have anything left at the finish. He vowed not to do the same thing a week later at the World

Championships in Oslo, Norway. The Tour de France may be cycling's most famous race, but the Worlds are almost as important to many riders. The title of world champion is one that every cyclist wants.

The race, 257 kilometers (160 miles) over fourteen laps, looked like it would be a problem for Lance. A heavy rain fell, drenching the competitors and making the course slippery. The conditions reminded Lance of his failure in his first professional race in Spain. But this time, the young American overcame the obstacle. He stayed in the front of the peloton throughout the first thirteen laps. He crashed twice, as did many of the riders, but was not hurt. After one crash, he fell far behind the peloton. But his teammates dropped back and joined him, helping him draft back to the lead pack.

On the final lap, as the riders approached the second-to-last climb, Lance knew it was time to attack. The leaders, including the Tour de France champion, Miguel Indurain, looked tired. They didn't seem ready for a strong push to the finish. But Lance was ready. He charged, and by the top of the climb, he had the tiniest of leads. He sped down the hill and pedaled hard into the final climb. He held his lead as he approached the final descent.

As he went down the hill at top speed, Lance knew the danger. At any moment, the bike's tires could lose their grip. He was risking a huge crash. But he didn't pull back at all. He was willing to risk it for the chance at the championship. "When I went, I knew I had to go with everything I had," he said. "It was all or nothing at that point—if I'd been caught, I wouldn't have had anything left for a sprint."

At one point, Lance looked over his shoulder to see how big his lead was. When he didn't see any other riders, he felt a moment of panic. Had he miscounted his laps? Had he attacked too soon, with another whole lap to go? If so, he would be doomed. But no, he hadn't miscounted. It was the final lap, and he was all alone. What Lance didn't know at the time was that his teammates had helped him again. They had ridden together to the front of the peloton and then slowed down, slowing down everyone else as well.

As he crossed the finish line, Lance started celebrating. He pumped his fists and jumped off the bike to hug his mother. He was the world champion, and there wasn't anyone else he wanted to celebrate with.

After the race, Lance heard that Norway's King Harald wanted to meet and congratulate the race winner. Lance and Linda went together to see the king. But when they approached the guard outside the king's room, their escort said that only Lance could enter. His mother would have to wait elsewhere.

Linda had sat outside in the pouring rain for the entire race. She had been a huge source of support for her son, and

Lance wasn't about to leave her behind. He took Linda by the arm and turned around. If they weren't going in together, he wasn't going in at all. As they walked away, the escort shouted after them. Linda could come too. Smiling, they entered to meet King Harald.

> “*Nobody has got [Lance's] intensity. Nobody. It's just phenomenal.*”
>
> —Chris Carmichael

Lance had made one of the highest achievements in cycling. But still, he thought about the Tour de France. That was how a cyclist really made his mark. The world's most famous cyclists had one thing in common—they were Tour champions. Lance wanted his name listed alongside Greg LeMond, Miguel Indurain, and Eddy Merckx.

But there was a problem. Lance wasn't a strong stage racer. He had done well in the Tour DuPont, but that race was nothing compared to the long, painful ordeal of the Tour de France. Some people didn't think Lance had the body to last the whole race. He was a big, muscular rider at 5 feet, 10 inches and 175 pounds. That build worked great for sprints. But in the Tour's long mountain stages, all the extra weight just slowed a rider down.

Lance had his doubts too, but he also had his dreams. He started training differently. He tried to slim down. He worked on his endurance. If he was going to take the next step in cycling, he needed to work hard. He was willing to do whatever it took to become a great stage racer.

The year 1994 was a time of transition for Lance. He kept improving. A second-place finish at the Clásica San Sebastián was a big moment for him—he hadn't forgotten his embarrassing last-place finish there in his first professional race. He also had some success at the Tour DuPont, winning one stage and finishing second overall to Russia's Viatcheslav Ekimov. But victories were hard to come by. Lance's backers and teammates sometimes grew impatient with his lack of results.

But Lance had a plan. In 1995 he targeted the Tour DuPont as a race he wanted to win. He'd finished second there twice. A win would help establish him as a real stage racer.

Lance struggled during the early stages of the race. But as the race moved into the mountains, he took control. He dominated the stage 4 climb and moved into first place by more than 2 minutes. He widened his lead the next day, winning the stage 5 time trial. This time, Lance never looked back. He won stage 9 and then cruised to a 2-minute victory over Ekimov. Once again, Lance's career was on the rise.

Chapter Five

Life and Death

Lance went to France in the summer of 1995 feeling good. Everything seemed to be going his way. He and his Motorola teammates were excited about the Tour de France, and this time, Lance intended to finish.

Fourteen days into the race, Lance was still riding strong. He knew he wasn't going to win the race, but that wasn't his goal. He just wanted to prove he could finish.

But everything changed on July 18, the day of stage 15. Lance was riding through a mountain pass, one of the steepest downhill sections of the race. In a descent like this one, riders go single file down the slope at speeds of more than 60 miles per hour. If one rider crashes, it can set up a bad chain reaction. That's what happened to a group ahead of Lance that day.

As Lance rode by, he saw there had been a crash. A large group of people was gathered around someone lying on the ground. Lance was speeding by, and he didn't know that the person was his teammate Fabio Casartelli. Casartelli, from Italy, had been one of about twenty riders involved in the crash. He had slammed his head into a concrete curb. Tour officials called for a helicopter to fly the injured cyclist to a hospital. But it was too late. Casartelli died in the helicopter.

A few minutes later, Lance learned what had happened to his friend and teammate. He was crushed and felt ill. But he had to finish the stage.

That night, Lance and the rest of the Motorola team had to decide what to do. Would they keep riding or quit the race? Lance wanted to stop racing. Suddenly, the Tour didn't seem important anymore. He didn't know if he had the will or desire to get back on his bike. But Fabio's wife talked to the team. She told them that her husband would want them to finish. So that's what they did.

The next day, for stage 16, the entire peloton rode together. No one tried to win. It was their way of honoring their lost friend. The racing could wait a day.

Stage 18 into the city of Limoges took on a new importance to Lance. Casartelli had been looking forward to that stage. He had hoped it would be his stage to win. Since his friend couldn't win it anymore, Lance decided to take Casartelli's place.

Halfway through the stage, Lance was riding with a group of about twenty-five cyclists. The race leader, Miguel Indurain, was heading the pack. The group slowly pulled away from the other riders. With about 40 kilometers (25 miles) to go, they hit a small descent. Lance didn't want to wait any longer. He charged. His attack came as a complete surprise to the other leaders. It was too early in the stage for a sprint to the finish. And a downhill attack was almost unheard of—it was dangerous and considered by most to be poor strategy. Lance's move didn't make any sense, and the other riders weren't sure what to do.

Lance took advantage of the confusion. In no time, he had a 30-second lead. The lead grew and grew. He finally crossed the finish line a full minute ahead of everyone else. As he crossed, he raised both arms, looked up, and pointed into the sky to honor his lost friend. He continued his tribute to Casartelli by completing the Tour, finishing in thirty-sixth place overall.

The tragedy at the 1995 Tour was hard on Lance, but other than that, his career was going great. The year 1996 started out as Lance's best year yet. The cycling world saw him as one of the sport's biggest stars. He won an important race in Belgium in the spring and then won the Tour DuPont again that summer.

Lance looked forward to the Tour de France, where he was finally considered a contender for the victory. He also hoped to win at the Olympics in Atlanta, Georgia. (By then, professionals were allowed to compete in the Olympic Games.) Lance didn't always feel his best, but he was training hard and still finishing well, so he didn't worry too much.

As the Tour de France got under way, things started to go wrong. Early in the race, heavy rains poured down on the cyclists. Lance pedaled on, but the effort took its toll on him. Soon he was coughing. His throat was sore. His back hurt. He couldn't keep going. Since the Olympics started just a few days after the Tour ended, Lance knew what he had to do. He dropped out of the Tour and tried to get himself healthy for the road race in Atlanta.

But that didn't work out, either. Lance still felt weak during the Olympics. He finished sixth in the time trial and struggled to twelfth in the road race. His body just couldn't give him what he needed. His muscles ached, and he was always sleepy.

A few bad finishes didn't slow down the demand for Lance Armstrong, though. He signed a contract worth $2.5 million to join a French racing team called Cofidis. At home in Texas, he moved into a mansion on the banks of Lake Austin. He had a boat, a sports car, and a swimming pool.

A few days after his twenty-fifth birthday that September, Lance and his friends were celebrating. But Lance had to leave the party early with a terrible headache. The headache got worse and worse, and there was nothing he could do to make it go away. "It was the kind of headache you see in the movies, a knee-buckling, head-between-your-hands, brain-crusher," Lance later wrote in his book *It's Not About the Bike.*

The headache wasn't his only problem. A few days later, he was coughing up blood. Then one of his testicles began to swell and hurt. He tried to ignore all these problems. He tried to keep training and pretend nothing was wrong. But he couldn't do it. Something *was* wrong. His doctor sent him to a specialist, Dr. Jim Reeves. Reeves wanted to run some tests to find out what was happening.

Lance lay on a table for more than an hour for a test called an ultrasound. When the test was done, the doctor told him he needed another test—a chest X-ray. That didn't make any sense to Lance. Why did they want to look at his chest? He was getting upset, but he did as he was told.

Lance returned to Reeves's office. It was getting late, and Lance knew the doctor normally would have gone home by then. That worried him.

Reeves looked at the X-rays, then looked at Lance. "This is a serious situation," he said. "It looks like testicular cancer."

Lance was shocked. *Cancer.* This wasn't just a danger to his career. It was a danger to his life.

Reeves explained more. He told Lance that the cancer had spread from his testicle to his lungs. It was possible to cure the cancer, but time was precious. The faster treatment started, the better Lance's chances would be. First of all, Lance needed surgery immediately to remove his testicle.

Cancer

Cancer is a disease in which some of the body's cells start growing out of control. The growing group of cells destroys normal cells, making the patient sick. To cure cancer, doctors have to kill the group of growing cells. But the drugs used to kill cancer cells end up killing many healthy cells as well.

Lance went home in a daze. He had to tell his friends and his mother. It was a tough night. But his friends supported him. They told him everything would be all right.

Early the next morning, Lance returned to the hospital for surgery. His friends filled the waiting room during the three-hour procedure. Finally, the good news came. The surgery had been a success. Lance was in a great deal of pain, but he was hopeful that the worst was behind him.

That hope quickly faded, though. More tests revealed that the cancer had spread more than previously thought. It was a stage-three cancer, meaning it had advanced a long way and would be harder to treat. For the next three months, Lance would need powerful chemotherapy (chemo), a kind of cancer treatment that can be very hard on the patient. The drugs used in the treatment kill cancer cells, but they also kill many healthy cells. Patients often lose a lot of weight. Their hair may fall out. It is a very unpleasant way to live. But without treatment, Lance would die. With the treatment, his chances of living were better than 60 percent.

Lance didn't let the treatments get him down. He tried to stay positive. His body handled the drugs without too many side effects. Once he was healed from the surgery, he even rode his bike a little every night.

> "*I don't know if I can ever get back to where I was—I don't know what this [cancer] is going to do to me. I want to come back and race—absolutely. But my priority is to live, and that's what I'm fighting for now. My second aim is to race again at the highest level.*"
>
> —LANCE ARMSTRONG

Lance talked to new doctors about his treatments. He wanted the doctors to use drugs that wouldn't destroy his muscles or hurt his chances of returning to cycling someday. But as his doctors worked, they didn't like the test results they got back. Something was still wrong. Lance's cancer wasn't going away. More bad news was on the way—the cancer had spread to Lance's brain. He had two tumors there.

When she found out, Linda broke down in tears. She knew what this news meant. Lance's chances of survival had just dropped—by a lot. Lance's doctors didn't say so at the time, but when they found the brain tumors, they thought his hopes of recovery were almost gone. The doctors told Lance that his chances for survival were about 50 percent. But that wasn't what they really thought. Privately, the doctors didn't expect him to live.

The next step for Lance was brain surgery. The idea was terrifying. The surgery could damage his vision and his coordination. If things went wrong, he would never ride again. But he had no choice. The tumors had to come out. He just had to hope for the best. So early on the morning of October 25, 1996, he went in for surgery. His doctor cut open a small part of his skull and removed the tumors. He was in surgery for six hours while his friends and family waited.

The surgery was a success. The tumors came out, and Lance's vision and coordination were not hurt. After recovering, Lance had to have more chemo. While Lance had done pretty well through his first batch of chemo, this one was harsher, and it was harder on him. But it was also the critical moment in his cancer treatment. If he was going to beat the cancer, it had to be then. If the cancer didn't respond, if the chemo didn't work, Lance would almost certainly die. Time after time, Lance had gotten more and more bad news. This time, he couldn't afford anything but good news.

> Because Lance had recently switched teams, he didn't have any employer-paid health insurance to cover the costs of his cancer treatment. He didn't just have to worry about his life. He also had to worry about losing everything he had to pay for the expensive treatments. But the Nike sporting goods company, one of his sponsors, found out about his troubles and got him added to its company health plan.

Lance's life revolved around his chemo. It was all he did. He was either getting a treatment or recovering from a treatment. He slept ten to twelve hours every night, his body exhausted by the battles going on inside it. He was ill, weak, and very tired. But he kept going. He told himself that the weakness and pain were signs that he was winning the battle.

By the end of the treatment, all he could do was lie curled up in a ball, retching. He noticed brown spots on his skin—they were chemo burns. The drugs were burning his body from the inside out.

Finally, the therapy was over. Lance had to wait to find out whether the drugs had killed off the cancer. The early tests were promising. It looked like the cancer was going away.

Lance was single-minded in beating his disease. He thought of it as a kind of race, a battle between him and cancer. "Cancer picked the wrong guy," he told a friend. "When it looked around for a body to hang out in, it made a big mistake when it chose mine."

Lance started riding his bike again. At first, he was weak. He had lost a lot of weight, most of it muscle. It was a struggle just to pedal along. But his strength slowly grew. Along with his strength grew his enthusiasm for joining the fight against cancer. He wanted to talk to other cancer patients and encourage them. He started the Lance Armstrong Foundation, based in Austin, to help fund the fight against cancer. To raise money for the foundation, he planned a charity bike race called the Ride for the Roses.

While he worked, he waited. His tests were good, and his doctors were hopeful that he would recover. But there was no way to be sure.

"The physical pain of cancer didn't bother me so much, because I was used to [pain]. In fact, if I didn't suffer, I'd feel cheated. The more I thought about it, the more cancer began to seem like a race to me. Only the destination had changed."

—LANCE ARMSTRONG

When Lance made a public announcement about his Ride for the Roses, he met a woman named Kristin "Kik" Richard. Richard worked in public relations and advertising. She was helping to promote the race. As Kik and Lance got to know each other better, they grew closer. Soon, they fell in love. It was an off-and-on romance at first. But in time, Lance had a new partner in his struggle to gain back his old life.

Chapter Six

Back on the Bike

About a year after his last chemo treatment, Lance got good news. His tests were still looking great. The doctors decided the fight was over. The cancer was gone. Lance had been cured.

It was fantastic news, putting an end to a long period of anxious waiting. But Lance had a new decision to make. Would he return to cycling? Could his body possibly ever take that kind of punishment again? When Lance saw a picture of himself winning a stage at the Tour de France, he felt like that part of his life was over. He told a friend that he'd never be able to compete again. But secretly, Lance never gave up hope. He didn't say so, but he still thought of himself as a cyclist.

In the summer of 1997, Lance and Kik went to Europe. Lance got to watch the Tour de France as a spectator. He also got to tour Europe in a way he never had as a cyclist. While he often thought about racing again, he also enjoyed not having to worry about competing.

As time went on, Lance thought more and more about coming back. Chris Carmichael constantly prodded him, encouraging him to start riding again. But Lance wasn't sure. Cancer and his treatment had changed him. He wasn't a strong 175 pounds anymore. Now he was a thin 158 pounds. He wouldn't have the same reserves of power that made him so fearsome on the road. Still, he wanted to find a way to compete again.

The Tour de France always finishes along the Champs-Elysées, a famous avenue in Paris. The road is also called *la plus belle avenue du monde,* which means "the most beautiful avenue in the world."

Finally, he made up his mind. He was going to start training again. He wanted to return for the 1998 season. He told his team, Cofidis, that he was on his way back. But he got a surprise. The team didn't want him anymore. It canceled his contract. Cofidis didn't believe Lance would ever be the rider he had been when it first signed him.

At first, the situation didn't seem like a big deal. Lance had been one of the rising stars of cycling before his illness. Surely, some other team would jump at the chance to sign him. But as Lance and his agent made call after call, they started to realize something. Nobody believed Lance could come back. Nobody wanted to sign him.

Finally, Lance found someone interested. An old friend, Thomas Weisel, was running a team sponsored by the U.S. Postal Service. Weisel had once owned the Subaru-Montgomery team, which Lance had signed with years before. Weisel was willing to take a chance on the comeback. Lance signed a contact for a low salary. But the contract included incentives, or bonuses. If Lance performed well, he would make up for the low salary with good bonus money. If not, he'd never make much money.

After Lance signed the contract, he wanted to celebrate with the woman he loved. He could think of no better way to do that than to propose. He bought a ring and asked Kik to marry him. She agreed. They planned a wedding for May 1998.

Everything seemed to be going Lance's way. He was training hard, trying to get back into shape. In February 1998, he rode in his first professional race since he had been diagnosed with cancer. The race was the Ruta del Sol, a five-day race in Spain. Lance didn't win the race, but his fourteenth-place finish proved that he was back.

While everyone marveled at his comeback, Lance still wasn't feeling confident. He wasn't the team leader anymore. Teammate George Hincapie was the featured U.S. Postal Service rider. Lance, like the other riders, was there to help Hincapie win. In his next race, called Paris-Nice for the route it runs between the two French cities, Lance discovered how frustrating not being the leader could be. The weather for the second stage was cold and rainy. Along the route, Hincapie had a flat tire. The entire team had to stop while he got his bike fixed. Then Lance and the other riders had to speed back to the peloton, wearing themselves out so Hincapie could save some energy.

As Lance started pedaling again, he was overcome with despair. Soon, he pulled over to the side of the road. He was done. He was quitting. And not just the race—he was quitting the entire comeback. He returned to Texas and told everyone he was retiring.

Lance's friends and family weren't sure what to do. They knew Lance wouldn't be happy if he quit. They wanted to get him back on the bike. They convinced him that he couldn't retire just yet. He had to wait until after the Ride for the Roses, his charity event. And they said he owed his U.S. fans a farewell race—the U.S. Pro Championships. Reluctantly, Lance agreed to compete in the two races. What he didn't know was that his friends and family were just stalling him. They thought that in time, he would change his mind.

Chris Carmichael convinced Lance to train for the Ride for the Roses. They went to Boone, North Carolina, where Lance had twice won the Tour DuPont. There, in the Appalachian Mountains, Lance started training again. And it was there, during a long ride and final climb, that he remembered why he loved cycling. He didn't want to quit anymore. He wanted to be a cyclist again.

> “*He realizes you've got to go for it, take big risks. You've got to seize it, and that's the way Lance is wired.*”
>
> —CHRIS CARMICHAEL

After his wedding in May, Lance got on his bike for the Ride for the Roses. It was a fun charity event, not a fierce professional race. Not surprisingly, Lance was the first rider across the finish line. He was ready for the U.S. Pro Championships. But it wouldn't be his farewell race, as he had once planned. It would be his second return to cycling. He finished fourth (his teammate George Hincapie won) and promptly decided that it was time to move back to Europe. He and Kik packed up and moved into a house in Nice, France.

Lance got immediate results. He won the Tour of Luxembourg, a four-day race, then finished fourth at the Tour of Holland, a weeklong race. His new, thinner build and fresh determination were making him a better stage racer than he'd been before the illness. But he still didn't have the strength to compete in the 1998 Tour de France.

Lance got back on the bike for the Tour of Spain, a hard three-week race and one of cycling's toughest events. This tour was a big test—would Lance have the strength to keep up with cycling's elite over such a long race? When he crossed the finish line in fourth place, a little more than 2 minutes behind winner Abraham Olano, Lance knew his body had passed the test. He was ready to become a top stage racer. A new goal emerged, one that had never really seemed possible until then. Lance wanted to win the Tour de France.

In Vitro Fertilization

Lance's cancer damaged his reproductive organs. To have children, he and Kik went through a process called in vitro fertilization (IVF). In this procedure, doctors removed eggs from Kik's body, fertilized the eggs in a laboratory, and then placed them back inside Kik's body.

This was his focus for 1999. Everything he did was in preparation for the Tour. When Kik learned in February that she was pregnant, the goal was even clearer. Lance was going to be a father, and there was no better way to support a family than by being the best cyclist in the world.

Lance started 1999 with a thud, though. He crashed at the Tour of Valencia and hurt his shoulder. A few weeks later, he was hit by a car during training. He finished second in the one-day Amstel Gold Race, losing to Michael Boogerd. But even this good showing was a disappointment. Boogerd was one of the favorites to win the 1999 Tour de France. Lance had badly wanted to beat Boogerd to prove to himself that he was in the elite class.

But the disappointments didn't make him lose focus. He and the U.S. Postal Service team trained even harder. Lance turned cycling into a science. He studied hard to determine the best strategies on each stage, each type of ride. He gained back some of the weight he had lost during his cancer treatments, but he made sure he stayed lean. He carefully controlled his diet, even weighing every ounce of food he ate.

Lance couldn't know how the Tour would play out, but he could be sure of one thing. If he lost, it wouldn't be for lack of preparation.

Chapter Seven

Comeback Complete

Finally, July arrived. Lance and his U.S. Postal Service team were in France, ready and anxious to get started. The team's director, Johan Bruyneel, had made Lance the team leader, believing that his power gave the team the best chance for a good finish. But few cycling experts paid much attention to a team led by a cancer survivor. Most people focused on the race favorites—Abraham Olano, Michael Boogerd, Miguel Indurain, Alexander Zulle, and Bobby Julich. Only one person, former champion Miguel Indurain, mentioned Lance's name as a possible winner.

Every Tour de France opens with a short, individual time trial called the Prologue. An all-out 8-kilometer (5-mile) sprint, the trial is important for the contenders. Nobody wants to get off to a poor start. The Tour is long and grueling enough without having to start out from behind.

As riders took off, the weather was perfect for racing. It didn't take long before Olano broke the Prologue record of 8:12 by 1 second. Shortly after that, Zulle broke the new record with a time of 8:07. Lance just wanted to stay with the lead group. As he crossed the finish line, he looked up at the clock. He was shocked by what he saw: 8:02—five seconds faster than Zulle and better than the old record by 10 seconds. For the first time in his life, he had earned the yellow jersey. The twenty-seven-year-old American was leading the Tour de France. He could hardly believe it.

Lance held on to the yellow jersey through stage 1 but lost it to Estonia's Jaan Kirsipuu the next day. He wasn't worried, though. The early stages of the Tour are in some ways just a warm-up for the brutal climbing stages at the end. The first part of the race takes place mainly on flat roads, which favor sprinters. But sprinters often fade during the climbing stages. All Lance had to do was stay with the leaders. His team rode in front of him, blocking the wind and giving him a good draft. They helped him stay up front without using up his legs too early.

During stage 2, a big crash slowed down many of the Tour's top contenders, including Boogerd and Zulle. Lance was in front of the mess. As the riders behind him slowed, he gained a big cushion over many of his most serious rivals.

© Stephen Dunn/Getty Images

As a teenager, Lance Armstrong competed in many triathlons. At age seventeen, he won the 1988 Jeep Triathlon Grand Prix.

© Mike Powell/Getty Images

Lance celebrates winning the fourth stage of the Tour DuPont in 1995.

Lance was proud to represent the United States at the 2000 Olympics in Sydney, Australia. Unfortunately, he wasn't in top condition and he took thirteenth place in the road race event and third in the time trial.

Lance shakes hands with Spaniard Alejandro Valverde *(center)* and German Jan Ullrich *(right)*. Lance considered Ullrich his main rival in the Tour de France.

Armstrong's amazing streak of wins in the Tour de France made him very popular with reporters.

In 2003 Lance crashed in stage fifteen of the Tour de France. He just barely won that year's Tour.

Lance Armstrong and rock star Sheryl Crow were a couple for a little more than two years. Here, they attend the 2005 American Music Awards together.

Lance's children, Luke, Isabella, and Grace, were among his biggest fans at the 2005 Tour de France.

Lance celebrates his final Tour de France victory with his teammates. Behind them is France's famous Arc de Triomphe.

Over the next week, Lance and his team did what they could to stay near the front. Lance didn't care too much about leading. He was saving his legs for the climbs. But by stage 8, he was ready to make a move. This 56.5-kilometer (35-mile) time trial around the city of Metz would be a great chance to make up time. Stage 8 also included two tough climbs, and Lance was eager to prove that he was a complete rider.

Special Jerseys

In the Tour de France, riders can earn several special jerseys. They are:

Yellow jersey: worn by the overall leader
Green jersey: worn by the best sprinter
Polka-dot jersey: worn by the best climber ("the King of the Mountains")
White jersey: worn by the best young rider

Lance started his time trial 2 minutes after Abraham Olano. When his turn to start finally came, he pedaled hard. He wanted to catch Olano and shake the Spaniard's confidence. This goal didn't take long to achieve. Early in the race, Olano crashed and lost a little time. Then Lance was on him. He blew by Olano, who had never before been passed in a time trial.

Lance was thrilled. But he wasn't done yet. He continued to stomp down on the pedals, putting up times that blew away the entire field. By the time he crossed the finish line, he had built a big lead, beating second-place Zulle by almost a minute. The yellow jersey was his again, and this time, he didn't want to give it back.

> "*I hope it sends out a fantastic message to all [cancer] survivors around the world. We can return to what we were before—and even better.*"
>
> —Lance Armstrong

Overall, the win gave Lance a lead of 2:20 over second-place Christophe Moreau of France. But Moreau wasn't a strong climber. The next real threat was Olano, 2:33 behind. A day off after the time trial allowed Lance to enjoy his lead. But he knew there was a lot of work to do. Stage 9 was the beginning of the true climbing stages. It was a 132-kilometer (82-mile) ride across six mountain passes. Many experts expected Lance to fade in the mountains. Early in his career, the climbs had been tough on him. Experts thought a more complete rider would catch him.

Lance wasted little time in proving that he wasn't going away. He worked with his teammates to draft throughout the early parts of the stage, saving his legs for a late attack. Soon, the weather turned cold, and rain began to fall. As the riders descended a peak, hailstones battered down on them. Several of Lance's teammates slowed. Another one crashed. Soon, Lance was without any help, riding with the world's best climbers. He fell behind the lead group. But he never let up. Alone, with nobody to turn to, Lance did the only thing he could think of—he attacked.

With 8 kilometers (5 miles) to go, Lance stood up and started pumping the pedals. After a half mile or so, he was within 10 seconds of the leaders. Once he could see them, he worked even harder. They looked back and saw the yellow jersey coming up fast. Still attacking, Lance sailed by and took the stage lead.

He kept going, wondering if the others had enough energy left to keep up. He wanted to crush their hopes, to show them they had no chance of catching him. His plan worked. The other riders couldn't match his pace. He pulled away, alone. Soon, no other riders were within sight. He crossed the finish line all by himself for a second straight stage win. More important, his lead over Olano had grown to an amazing 6 minutes.

Despite his great success, Lance still had his critics. Reporters questioned how a man who had been a cancer patient only a few years before could possibly be leading such a grueling sporting event. He had never been a contender before the cancer, the critics noted. Why was he so good all of a sudden? Some people suspected that Lance was doping—using steroids or other performance-enhancing drugs. Lance told his critics that he had never used illegal drugs. Every drug test proved that he was "clean"—or drug free.

> Lance's U.S. Postal Service teammates gave him a nickname, Mellow Johnny, because it sounds like *maillot jaune,* the French words for "yellow jersey."

For the rest of the Tour, Lance's huge lead was a big advantage. He didn't really need to attack anymore. He just had to stay with the peloton and not let anyone jump out too far ahead. By the end of stage 13, his lead was 7:44. He continued his conservative approach, just riding along and staying out of trouble.

At the end of stage 15, Lance was riding at the front with Spaniard Fernando Escartín. The stage ran along France's border with Spain, so Escartín badly wanted to win. The Spaniard attacked hard, quickly pulling away from Lance. Lance could have tried to keep up, but he didn't *have* to keep up. He crossed the finish line more than 2 minutes behind Escartín. Even so, Lance wasn't worried. Escartín had moved into second place overall, but he was still a whopping 6:19 behind Lance.

By this time, the rest of the Tour was a formality. "Armstrong is the strongest. He's going to win the Tour, no question," said Alexander Zulle. "He is in control over every situation. . . . It's been like that for two weeks."

Lance had one more goal. The Tour includes three individual time trials. Lance had won the first two. Only three riders had ever won all three. Lance wanted to match their feat by winning stage 19 on the second-to-last day of the Tour. Some people advised him to take it easy, not to push. But his mind was made up. He was going for the sweep. "The time trials are . . . the race of truth," he said. "It would have been easy to go 90 percent, but I wanted to prove the [rider with the] yellow jersey is the strongest one in the race."

Lance started off fast, with the best time at each of the first two checkpoints. But as he approached the end of the 57-kilometer (35-mile) course, his legs grew tired. Despite his aching muscles, he pedaled harder, faster. He crossed the finish line with a time of 1:08:17—9 seconds better than second-place Zulle. Lance had done it—he had won stage 19 and swept the time trials. It was his way of putting an exclamation point on his Tour win.

The final day, stage 20, was almost like a celebration parade for Lance. By tradition, the peloton doesn't do any real racing during most of the 89-kilometer (55-mile) stage. They don't start riding fast until they see the famous Eiffel Tower of Paris. Lance was relaxed as he rode. He did interviews through his radio headset. He even ate an ice cream cone on his bike.

As he pedaled over the cobblestones of a street called the Champs-Elysées, the crowd cheered. Spectators waved Texan and American flags all along the course. After he crossed the finish line as the winner, Lance ran to hug Kik and his mom. He was overjoyed. He had accomplished what had seemed almost impossible—he had beaten cancer and returned to cycling as a better racer than he had been before the illness. "This is an awesome day," he said. "This is beyond belief."

> "*To win the Tour de France [after cancer] is mind-boggling. Just to enter is incredible. It could not have happened to a better person.*"
>
> —Dr. Lawrence Einhorn, one of Lance's doctors

Even though most Americans don't following cycling, Lance was an instant hit back in the United States. His good looks and positive attitude, along with his inspirational victory over cancer, made him an irresistible story. He was in high demand, appearing on *Late Night with David Letterman, Today,*

Larry King Live, and other TV shows. New sponsors wanted to sign him to endorsement deals. He agreed to write an autobiography. Everybody wanted a piece of Lance Armstrong.

The good news kept coming. That October, Lance was giving a speech in Las Vegas, Nevada, when he got a phone call from Kik. She told him she was going into labor, the beginning stages of having their baby. Lance was surprised. She wasn't due to give birth for two more weeks. But he quickly got on a flight back home. After a difficult delivery, Luke David Armstrong was born on October 12, 1999. Lance and Kik were parents.

Everything was going perfectly. Lance had conquered his past. In the present, he was the world's best cyclist. And his future seemed secure with his infant son.

Chapter Eight

Defending the Title

Despite all his success, Lance still felt he had something to prove. Some experts in the cycling world discounted his 1999 Tour victory. They thought his victory might be a fluke—a stroke of luck—and that he could never repeat it. They pointed out that 1997 champion Jan Ullrich and 1998 champion Marco Pantani had missed the 1999 Tour and how they might have beaten Lance if they'd been there.

To counter the criticism, Lance focused only on the Tour. All the other races faded in importance for him. They were just warm-ups. All that mattered was the Tour de France and proving that his win hadn't been a fluke.

Doubt about Lance's ability to repeat only grew in the spring of 2000. He was practicing with the U.S. Postal Service team on a hot day in the Pyrenees. As Lance sped down a slope, he hit a small rock that blew out his front tire. He lost control of the bike and sailed into a brick wall that ran alongside the road. He hit the wall headfirst and briefly lost consciousness.

It was a violent and terrifying crash. Lance's teammates rushed to help their leader. But Lance had a bit of very good luck on his side. Two tourists had been sitting nearby. Both of them were doctors. They rushed to his side. "From the sound of his head hitting the wall, I was 100 percent sure I would walk over here and find a dead man," said one of the doctors.

Lance wasn't dead, though. He was rushed to the nearest hospital, treated, and released. He was banged up and bruised, but that was all. He'd be all right. After a few days' rest, he was back on the bike, training again. By the time July came, he was ready.

Jan Ullrich

Over the years, German Jan Ullrich has been Lance's biggest rival. Ullrich finished second in the 1996 Tour de France—his first time in the race. When Ullrich won the Tour in 1997, many believed he would go on to break the record of five Tour victories. Lance has always considered Ullrich his main competition.

The 2000 Tour de France would be very different from the race Lance had won the year before. The competitors—including

Ullrich and Pantani—would be tougher. The course would be different and more difficult. Race officials had decided to have the course run counterclockwise, the opposite direction of the previous year. The new direction created some very difficult stages.

Lance got an immediate reminder that repeating wouldn't be easy. He finished second in the opening, 16-kilometer (10-mile) time trial. He was only 2 seconds behind leader David Millar, but Lance knew he had work to do.

Through the early stages, Lance and his teammates just tried to stay in the pack. They were confident that they could build a lead in the mountains. The goal early on was to stay out of trouble and avoid crashes. By the end of stage 9, Lance was in sixteenth place.

Stage 10—in the Pyrenees—was where the race would really begin for Lance. The stage included a brutal 13-kilometer (8-mile) climb. Lance knew the climb would bury most of the riders in front of him. He got on his bike on a cold and windy morning knowing that this was his day to claim the yellow jersey.

Early in the stage, Spaniard Javier Otxoa began an attack. It was a bizarre move, far too early in the race. But Otxoa built a huge lead, leaving Lance and the other riders wondering what to do. They decided to let him go. As Lance approached the long climb, he stayed in a pack with Zulle, Ullrich, and Pantani.

Not long into the climb, Pantani attacked. But Lance wouldn't let him go. He stayed on the Italian's back wheel, not giving up an inch. While the others tired, Lance kept attacking. Soon, he was behind only Otxoa. With 5 kilometers (3 miles) to go, Lance was 5 minutes behind the Spaniard. With 2 kilometers (1.2 miles) left, Lance had cut the lead to just over 2 minutes. Otxoa was tired.

Honorable Riders

It's a tradition in the Tour de France for riders to wait for someone who has crashed—especially a leader. In 2001 Lance stopped to wait for Jan Ullrich to get up from a bad crash. Ullrich returned the favor a few years later when Lance was on the pavement.

Lance kept attacking, hoping he could make up the time. But Otxoa had enough energy to hold off the American and win the stage. Lance was disappointed not to get the stage win. It was still a good day, though. He'd beaten his serious rivals and pulled into the overall lead, earning the yellow jersey for the first time since riding into Paris the year before.

The lead continued to grow in the mountains. The only real trouble Lance had came at the end of stage 12, at Mont Ventoux. He was riding at the front of the pack with Pantani. The two cyclists were battling for the stage lead. But shortly before the finish line, Lance stopped his attack. He was confident in his overall lead, so he let Pantani win the stage.

His decision angered Pantani. He thought Lance was just showing off by letting someone else win. "I don't need to be given a gift from Armstrong," Pantani said. "The Tour is not over. If Armstrong thinks it's finished, he's mistaken. In any case he isn't finished with me."

By stage 16, even Pantani knew that he wouldn't catch Lance. So he took out his anger in a different way—by trying to wear out the twenty-eight-year-old Texan. Pantani made an early attack and built a huge stage lead. He wasn't trying to win, though. He knew that as the leader, Lance would have to try to keep up. Pantani just wanted to wear Lance down so other riders could gain time. His plan worked—both riders ran out of energy before the end of the stage. The peloton passed them, and Lance lost more than a minute and a half of his lead to Ullrich. After the stage, Pantani withdrew from the race.

In the end, Pantani's attack didn't really hurt Lance. He quickly built his lead back and showed that nobody was going to catch him. By stage 19, a time trial, only one goal remained. Lance wanted to win a stage. Despite his comfortable lead, he hadn't done that yet in 2000.

Ullrich, still in second place, started the time trial 3 minutes before Lance. Ullrich was a big crowd favorite because the stage went through part of his home country of Germany. Fans also wanted to see him cut into Lance's lead to make the final stages more interesting. But at each checkpoint, Lance's times were better. He wasn't going to lose ground to Ullrich. He crossed the finish line 25 seconds faster than his rival to earn the stage win and increase his overall lead to more than 6 minutes.

> “*In the hardest part of the race, Lance reveals an unbending will, uncommon determination, and unquestioned courage. He has shown that courage in sport. He has also shown that courage in life.*”
>
> —President George W. Bush, 2001

"I really wanted to win this stage," he said. "I had a lot of stress and a lot of anger and a lot of pressure. The Tour wouldn't be complete for me . . . without winning a stage."

Again, the final stages were just a formality. Lance rode across the finish line of stage 21 in Paris with a glass of champagne in his hand. When the race was over, he stood on the podium with Kik and nine-month-old Luke. "This one's even more special than last year, partly because of this little guy," Lance said, holding Luke.

Lance didn't spend much time celebrating. He needed to prepare for his next big race, at the 2000 Olympics in Sydney,

Australia. He had been disappointed with both of his Olympic finishes before. This time, he wanted gold.

But again, a crash in training hurt his chances. Riding around a sharp turn, Lance ran into a car. He flew off his bike headfirst, onto the ground. The next day, he went to a doctor, who told him he'd broken a bone in his neck.

> "*No one automatically gives you respect just because you show up. You have to earn it.*"
>
> —Lance Armstrong

Lance rested for a few days, then got back to training. The injury was painful, but Lance stayed in shape. By the time he got to Sydney, he was well enough to compete. But he still wasn't 100 percent, and it showed. He took thirteenth place in the road race event and third in the time trial. Third place got him a bronze medal, but Lance was disappointed. He'd had his heart set on gold.

Lance's life didn't get any easier in November 2000. On Thanksgiving Day, French officials announced that they were launching a criminal investigation into Lance—and his U.S. Postal Service teammates—for illegal drug use. Lance was absolutely shocked. The only evidence the French officials had was a bag of garbage that team doctors had thrown away. Because the garbage hadn't been disposed of in the usual place, investigators suspected that it contained something the team didn't want found.

The team denied all the reports. Lance insisted that he'd never used performance-enhancing drugs. He said the idea was absurd—that he would never risk his health by using dangerous drugs after fighting so hard for his life only a few years earlier. But the rumors only grew more widespread. To make matters worse, Greg LeMond, the most successful American cyclist, publicly criticized Lance, suggesting that the drug use accusations were true. LeMond's remarks hurt Lance.

Life in France became increasingly difficult. The French fans had never really liked Lance in the first place. They considered cycling their sport, and they didn't want Americans coming in and dominating it. On top of that, the scandal was everywhere. The media constantly hung out around Lance's home in Nice, even when he was off training and Kik was there alone. Reporters dug through his garbage, hoping to find some evidence of guilt. Soon, Lance couldn't take it anymore. He and Kik moved to nearby Girona, Spain.

But it wasn't just the media causing problems. Sponsors began to back away from Lance and his teammates. They didn't want to be associated with any athletes that were thought of as cheaters. It didn't matter that there was no proof. Many people had already made up their minds that Lance was guilty.

The French courts requested all the urine samples that Lance had provided for earlier drug tests. The court's scientists checked the samples over and over, searching for proof of drug use. They could never find any. But the scientists still wouldn't clear Lance's name. They checked the samples again. The investigation dragged on and on. In the end, the court decided what Lance knew all along. There was no proof Lance had done anything wrong.

> During the final stage of the 2000 Tour, Lance had some fun with the fans. He wore a long, black wig and took pictures of the crowd as he pedaled by.

In April 2001, Lance and Kik got some much-needed good news. Kik was pregnant again. The couple later learned that she would have twins. The family was growing fast.

Things got even better in July, when Lance staged his amazing come-from-behind victory in the 2001 Tour de France, erasing a 35-minute deficit in only a few days. It was an extra-special win for Lance because he wanted to make a statement to the fans and race officials who had doubted him during the doping investigation. Lance was a three-time Tour champion and the best stage racer in the world. How long could he keep going? Only Lance could answer that question.

Chapter Nine

Cycling Legend

After his recovery, Lance worried whether the cancer was really gone from his body. He lived in fear that the disease would come back. In October 2001, a few months after his third-straight Tour victory, Lance made a trip to his doctor for tests. It was the five-year anniversary of his cancer diagnosis—a major date for a cancer survivor. If cancer hasn't returned after five years, doctors consider the patient to be completely cancer free. Lance got that news from his doctor. The cancer was gone, and it wasn't likely to ever come back.

More good news came in November when Kik gave birth to twin girls, Isabelle and Grace. Everything seemed perfect. But with three small children and a busy cycling schedule, Lance and Kik had difficulty making time for themselves. They didn't talk as much anymore. They were both so wrapped up in their lives that they began to grow apart.

Lance was growing even closer to his teammates, however. The U.S. Postal Service team had earned the nickname Big Blue for the blue jerseys the team members wore. Lance's three straight Tour wins had made the once little-known team into a powerhouse. He was surrounded by good teammates—cyclists who knew what it took to work as a team. They were willing to work and sweat to give their leader any advantage.

Wearing Blue

To start the 2002 Tour, Lance wore a regular blue team jersey. Traditionally, the defending champion begins the race in the yellow jersey. But Lance wanted to send a message to his teammates and to himself—if U.S. Postal wanted the jersey, they had to earn it all over again.

Their dedication to Lance and to the team showed again in the 2002 Tour. Lance was trying to become only the fourth rider in Tour history to win a fourth-straight title. If he could do it, he would join an elite list of riders—Jacques Anquetil, Eddy Merckx, and Miguel Indurain.

The 2002 Tour promised to be a new challenge for Lance. Tour officials didn't like how he had dominated in the past three races. They felt the last few stages were too boring, since everyone already knew who would win. Officials wanted to make the final stages more exciting. They changed the course so that many tough climbs came at the end. Lance would need his team's help more than ever.

The race started out perfectly, with Lance winning the opening time trial. He didn't hold on to the yellow jersey, though, knowing better than to try to keep up with the sprinters. He would wait for the mountains to get the jersey back. Again, he just wanted to stay out of trouble early on.

But trouble found Lance. During stage 7, he was caught up in a small crash. A teammate was bumped from behind and lost his balance. As he went down, his handlebars got caught in the spokes of Lance's rear tire. The team needed more than a minute to get back up and racing. The accident dropped Lance from third place to eighth.

After a disappointing second-place finish in the stage 9 time trial, Lance came back in stage 11, a long and difficult climb over three peaks. Lance's teammates took turns leading him up the mountain, allowing him to draft and save energy. Finally, Lance was ready to attack. He rode at the front with Spain's Joseba Beloki, his main competition in the Tour. But he just couldn't leave the Spaniard behind. With about 200 meters (660 feet) to go, Lance made his move. Beloki couldn't keep up, and Lance crossed the finish line first, 7 seconds ahead. Lance had won the stage and took over the yellow jersey.

Big Blue kept pushing. The team seemed unstoppable in the mountains. Stage after stage, Lance increased his lead. Soon, he was four and a half minutes ahead of Beloki. Lance added a win at the stage 18 time trial and again cruised into Paris with victory.

By tradition, the Tour winner gives a big chunk of his winnings (totaling about $400,000) to his teammates. Lance was so grateful for all the help he'd been given that he doubled the usual amount. He wanted to keep his teammates happy and make sure they stayed with the team. He was already thinking about a fifth-straight title in 2003.

Lance Armstrong's name was bigger than ever, and he continued to use it to call attention to the fight against cancer. At the end of 2002, he received one of the highest honors in sports when the magazine *Sports Illustrated* named him Sportsman of the Year.

Lance kept training hard. But as he did, the problems in his marriage grew. In February 2003, he and Kik separated. They wanted to spend some time apart to think about their marriage. It was a tough step. But because cyclists are often separated from their families, Lance was used to living on his own. He missed Kik and the children, but he threw his full attention into his training.

As the 2003 Tour approached, Lance had a streak of bad luck. During a warm-up race, the thirty-one-year-old Lance crashed and hurt his hip. The week before the Tour, he got sick. A day before the race started, he still wasn't feeling well. In the Prologue, he finished a disappointing seventh. In stage 1, he went down in a crash, which left him with scrapes and bruises. He had to borrow a teammate's bike to finish the stage.

Team Player

Lance liked to reward his teammates for all the help they gave him. In some non-Tour races, he let his teammates lead, helping them win races the same way they helped him during the Tour.

Fans and other riders began to wonder if age had finally caught up with Lance Armstrong. Were his best racing days behind him? Was this the year his reign as champion would end? Jan Ullrich and others were eager to find out.

Throughout the early stages, Lance and his teammates used the same strategy they used every year—they just wanted to stay close to the leaders. They fought through very hot weather and long, flat courses, waiting for the mountain stages.

One highlight for the team was winning stage 4, the team time trial. During this event, team members ride as a group. Everyone on the team earns the same time for the stage. U.S. Postal had often struggled in the event in past years.

Stage 8 was the first major climb into the Alps. In earlier years, Lance had dominated this part of the race. But this time he struggled with fatigue, and his opponents saw an opening. Finally, more than halfway through the 219-kilometer (136-mile) stage, Lance realized why he was so tired. His back brake was rubbing against the wheel. He was riding uphill with his brake on!

Lance fixed the problem and picked up speed. But his fourth-place finish was a disappointment, even though it was fast enough to give him the yellow jersey. Of bigger concern was his energy level. How much had all that extra work pedaling with the brake on cost his body? Only time would tell.

Lance had another scare in the next stage. Joseba Beloki, who started the day in second place, crashed while trying to make a turn. To avoid running into Beloki, Lance had to steer off the road. He didn't know what was waiting off the road. It could have been a cliff or a big rock. But he was lucky—he sailed into an open field. He kept going, pedaling through the field, looking for a place to get back on the road. But before he could do so, he came upon a big ditch. He had to carry his bike over it. Finally, he got back on the road and hurried to catch up with the leaders. Beloki was not as lucky. He suffered several broken bones and had to withdraw from the race.

In the stage 12 time trial, Lance had more problems. He ran out of water on a brutally hot day. Tour rules don't allow riders to get any help during time trials, so no one could give Lance the drink he badly needed. Ullrich, still Lance's biggest rival for the championship, gained more than a minute and a half during the 47-kilometer (29-mile) stage.

"I had an incredible crisis," Lance said after the stage. "I felt like I was pedaling backward." And although Lance held on to the yellow jersey with a slim lead, Ullrich had more reason than ever to believe that Lance's Tour dominance might be over.

Lance struggled again in stage 13. His body had lost a lot of water, and he still hadn't fully recovered. Ullrich closed in, pulling within 15 seconds of the overall lead. But despite everything that had gone wrong, Lance was still wearing the yellow jersey at the end of the stage.

After Lance and Ullrich finished stage 14 side by side, the lead was still 15 seconds. By then, Lance was feeling better. He knew that only a few stages remained. He needed to make a move before the race left the mountains.

But Ullrich was confident. He'd seen Lance at his worst and told the media that he'd have the lead by the end of stage 15.

The comments motivated Lance. He set off to win the stage and build the kind of comfortable lead he was used to.

Early in the stage, Ullrich made an attack. Lance didn't try to go with him, though, knowing how much more riding was to come. Lance was right—Ullrich couldn't keep up the speed, and the lead group quickly caught back up to him.

As the cyclists reached the final climb of the stage, Lance saw that Ullrich had dropped behind the pack. He'd worn himself out with the early attack. Lance saw his opportunity. He stood up on his pedals and charged. He was pulling away. He thought he would take control of the Tour again and leave all his bad luck behind.

> “*Armstrong's courageous, a fighter. Somebody who perseveres until the end.*”
>
> —Bernard Hinault, five-time Tour de France champion

As he attacked, he saw a fan in front of him. The young boy was swinging a yellow bag. By the time Lance saw the danger, it was too late. The bag caught his handlebar. In an instant, Lance was falling over sideways, smashing his right side on the pavement and scraping his elbow. For a moment, he thought he might be seriously injured. His hip hurt. He briefly wondered if he'd be able to continue or whether this was how his quest for a fifth championship would end.

He wasn't going to go down that easily, though. He got up and jumped back on his bike. "After the fall, I had a big, big rush of adrenaline," he said.

Superior Preparation

Reporters often asked Lance when he started training for each upcoming Tour de France. He always gave the same answer: the morning after the previous Tour ended. He believed that superior preparation, not superior ability, was what made him a champion.

After a few minutes, he was ready to resume his attack. Again, he pulled away. Ullrich and the other riders simply couldn't keep up with the furious climb. Lance crossed the finish line alone. He had extended his lead over Ullrich to 1:07 with five stages to go. But bleeding and exhausted, he didn't even celebrate his stage win. "This has been a Tour of too many problems, too many close calls," he said. "I wish it would stop. I wish I could just have some uneventful days."

For the next three stages, Lance and Ullrich rode together, neither able to gain much time. With two stages left, Lance's lead was 1:05. Stage 19 would be the key. Ullrich had to gain a big chunk of time to have any chance entering the final stage. But as hard as he tried, Ullrich couldn't cut into the lead. In fact, Lance added another 11 seconds to the margin, pretty much assuring himself another title.

When no disasters came in stage 20, the race was over. Lance Armstrong had again won the Tour de France. The title was his fifth, tying him with four others—Jacques Anquetil, Eddy Merckx, Bernard Hinault, and Miguel Indurain—for the most Tour wins ever. Indurain was the only other rider to have won five in a row.

"It's a dream, really a dream," Lance said. "I love cycling, I love my job and I will be back for a sixth. It's incredible to win again."

Chapter Ten

Record Setter

After his 2003 Tour victory, Lance took some time away from cycling. He promoted his new book, *Every Second Counts.* He also took part in charity events, did interviews, and appeared on talk shows.

Lance and Kik also tried to get back together during this time. But by September, they decided that the marriage wasn't working and announced that they would divorce. Despite the breakup of their marriage, Lance and Kik remained friends. They lived near each other in Austin and shared custody of their children.

Not long after the divorce, Lance had a new woman in his life. He began to date rock singer Sheryl Crow, whom he met at a charity event in Las Vegas. "We're very similar," Lance said. "She likes to stay busy. She's always on, and I like that. . . . When we're together, we never feel bothered or uncomfortable."

Despite the changes in his personal life, Lance managed to focus on his only real goal for 2004—winning a record sixth Tour de France. Nobody had ever done it. He was excited to be going back to France with his U.S. Postal Service team.

Lance the Author

Lance worked with Sally Jenkins to write two books. The first was an autobiography titled *It's Not About the Bike.* It was published in 2000. In 2003 Lance and Jenkins published a second book, *Every Second Counts.*

In the Prologue, Lance finished second to Switzerland's Fabian Cancellara. But he finished 15 seconds ahead of Jan Ullrich and his other main challengers. Rain and bad weather followed the Tour throughout the early stages, so more than ever, Lance's goal was just to stay out of trouble. He dropped several places in the standings, but he wasn't worried.

Stage 4 was the team time trial. After winning this event in 2003, Lance's team had high hopes. A steady rain had fallen for much of the day, but the weather finally let up as Big Blue was making its run. The combination of improved weather and good strategy gave the U.S. Postal Service team the win and helped

Lance gain the yellow jersey for the first time in the 2004 Tour.

Other riders attacked early in stage 6, but Lance didn't try to chase them. The mountains were still a week away, and he didn't plan to hold the yellow jersey until then. He was content to finish back in the pack. He lost the lead and fell to sixth place, more than 9 minutes behind leader Thomas Voeckler.

Lance held that place over the next several stages, flat courses that favored sprinters. He stayed near Voeckler, riding and waiting. Entering stage 12, he was 9:35 back. But the mountains had come.

Heavy rains fell on the peloton as it entered the Pyrenees. It was perfect weather for Lance and his teammates, who were used to practicing in such conditions. On the final climb, they made a serious attack. Voeckler couldn't keep up. Their blistering pace took its toll on many strong competitors, including Jan Ullrich and Lance's former teammate Tyler Hamilton.

Only Ivan Basso, an Italian rider and Lance's good friend, was able to keep up. Basso's mother was fighting cancer, and the two riders had formed a close bond. As the two approached the stage's finish line, everyone expected Lance to make a mad sprint to the finish. But he didn't. He fell in behind Basso and took second place out of respect for his friend.

The two men were again side by side as they chased the stage 13 finish. They worked together to set a pace that their rivals couldn't maintain. But this time, Lance wasn't content with second. He sprinted to the finish for the win, his first stage victory of the 2004 Tour. The win moved him into second place overall, 22 seconds behind Voeckler. Basso was third, 1:39 back.

Lance's next move came in stage 15. Voeckler fell back with a flat tire. Lance knew this was his chance to take back control of the race. With a burst of energy at the end, Lance barely beat Basso and Ullrich for the stage win. More important, he had the yellow jersey back with a lead of 1:25 over Basso.

Lance and his teammates were happy to have the lead, but they were also worried. Basso was riding well. Lance didn't have much margin for error. A minute and a half just wasn't a comfortable lead.

Stage 16 was a time trial—Lance's best chance to extend his lead. Basso wasn't strong in time trials, while Lance had always excelled there. Sure enough, Lance took advantage of the opportunity. He was the last to start, 2 minutes after Basso. Lance caught the Italian with about 3 kilometers (1.9 miles) to go. He won the stage by more than a minute over Ullrich and increased his overall lead to 3:48 over Basso. With four stages left, Lance's pursuit of a record sixth-straight victory seemed almost assured.

But Lance wasn't done dominating the race. He won again the next day, the 204-kilometer (127-mile) climb of stage 17.

Then he won again in stage 19, the final time trial. Lance had another huge lead entering the final stage and crossed the finish line without much drama. He had done what no other cyclist had ever done—he'd won six Tours. He'd also set another record. At age thirty-two, he was the oldest winner in the race's history.

As he stood on the podium after the race, "The Star-Spangled Banner" played over the loudspeakers. The next song was "All I Wanna Do (Is Have Some Fun)," one of Sheryl Crow's biggest hits.

Lance enjoyed the victory with his teammates, knowing the next year would be one of change. It was the last time Lance would wear his U.S. Postal Service jersey. The team's sponsorship was changing. The Discovery Channel was taking over as sponsor, although the team members remained the same.

In 2004 Lance was named the Associated Press Male Athlete of the Year—for the third-straight year!

Lance stayed in the headlines throughout the rest of 2004 and the early part of 2005. Nike and the Lance Armstrong Foundation started a new fund-raising effort called WEARYELLOW

LIVESTRONG. The foundation sold yellow wristbands for $1 apiece to raise money for cancer research. The campaign, along with other fundraisers, raised $50 million in one year.

Lance also was in the headlines as his relationship with Sheryl grew. News photographers loved to take pictures of the famous couple. And Lance still could not escape doping rumors.

As the 2005 Tour approached, reporters wanted to know Lance's future plans. Finally, on April 18, 2005, Lance made a statement. "I have decided the [2005] Tour de France will be my last race as a professional cyclist," he said. "Ultimately, athletes have to retire . . . the body doesn't just keep going and going."

> Lance made a short appearance in the 2004 movie *Dodgeball: A True Underdog Story.* In the movie, he plays himself. He convinces the lead character to keep trying and not to quit.

Lance already had the record. His name was forever sealed as one of the greatest cyclists in history. Whether he finished first, last, or anywhere in between in the 2005 Tour wouldn't change that. But Lance wanted to go out as a winner. He wanted his final race to be a celebration of his whole career. The only way to do that was to win.

As always, Lance and his teammates trained hard. Nothing less than victory would be acceptable. As he had for years, he treated many of the spring races as tune-ups. His vision was focused on that final Tour. Finally, July came. Lance made his last trip to France as a competitor. All the attention was focused on him as he sat on his bike before the Prologue, the last of 189 riders, waiting for his signal to start.

But his quest for a seventh Tour championship started with a sputter. His foot slipped off his pedal. He quickly got it back on and took off riding. Before long, he had Jan Ullrich (who had started a minute earlier) in sight. He passed the German and cruised to a second-place finish. His lead over Ullrich was 1:06.

Lance used his usual early-race strategy by riding with the pack and staying out of trouble. The Discovery Channel team won the team time trial in stage 4. But in stage 8, the first stage in the mountains, where Lance liked to turn up the heat, he found himself in real trouble. A group of riders set a blistering pace, determined to isolate the thirty-three-year-old American. The plan worked—Lance's teammates couldn't keep up the pace. Soon, he was alone, without any help.

Lance kept fighting, though. He couldn't win the stage, but he managed to finish in a pack only 27 seconds behind the leaders. The day had taken a heavy toll on his legs, and he'd missed the opportunity to take control of the race. But he'd survived.

Only two stages later, Lance had a new chance to take control. Stage 10 was the first of several brutal climbs—exactly the sort of stage Lance could use to build a huge lead on his rivals. This time, there were no mistakes. He made a big attack that Jan Ullrich, Ivan Basso, and the other competitors couldn't match. He finished the stage second, with an overall lead of 38 seconds over Mickael Rasmussen.

George Hincapie

Born in Queens, New York, in 1973, George Hincapie is the only teammate to have ridden at Lance's side in each of his seven Tour de France victories. He began racing at age ten and first made headlines in 1990, when he put together seventeen straight junior victories. In 2005 he won Stage 15 of the Tour de France, his first stage victory after ten years of competing.

As the stages passed by, the lead slowly grew. By the end of stage 19, his lead was 2:46 over Basso. With only two stages to go, it was a very comfortable lead. But something was missing. Not counting the team time trial, Lance still hadn't won a stage. He wanted to change that with the stage 20 time trial—the last time trial in his amazing career.

Lance rode with purpose. He went hard and blew the field away on the 55-kilometer (34-mile) course. When he crossed the finish line, he'd won the stage by 23 seconds over Ullrich and increased his overall lead to more than 4 minutes.

Stage 21 marked the end of the Tour and the last ride of Lance's professional career. Because of severe weather, officials declared Lance the winner with about 48 kilometers (30 miles) still to go. For Lance, the ride into Paris was a long victory parade. As he crossed the finish line, his career as a professional cyclist ended. Lance Armstrong had won his seventh-straight Tour de France, a feat that might never be matched.

> *"Lance wants to win the Tour, only the Tour. The rest [of the races] mean nothing to him."*
>
> —Jean-Marie Leblanc, director, Tour de France

"It's nice to finish your career on a high note," Lance had said the day before, knowing that his Tour victory was assured. "As a sportsman, I wanted to go out on top."

Epilogue

Moving On

After Lance's victory in the 2005 Tour de France, he stood on the podium with his three children. The crowd cheered. His son, Luke, looked uncomfortable in front of all the people. He asked Lance if they could go home.

For once, Lance could finally answer yes. He was ready to go home. He was eager to go back to Texas and be a dad. He also looked forward to more time with Sheryl. In September 2005, he proposed to her, and she agreed to marry him.

A few months later, Lance and Sheryl called off their engagement. They said they continued to have great respect for each other, and it was a difficult decision for both of them. Fortunately for Lance, he had some happier news to focus on—he had been named Associated Press Male Athlete of the Year for the fourth-straight year. It was one more record-setting accomplishment for the newly retired cyclist.

Lance's retirement allowed him to do more work with the Lance Armstrong Foundation and the LIVESTRONG program, which had sold more than 50 million wristbands. He also had time for new activities. He talked about possibly running for political office someday.

Asked if he would ever consider a return to cycling to chase yet another Tour victory, Lance said, "Now that we have number seven, number eight doesn't really make a difference. It's time for me to move on with my life."

Lance planned to keep working with his old team, consulting with coaches and riders, helping them build a new identity and a new winning tradition. At the same time, he looked forward to leaving the intense world of professional cycling behind for a little while.

But the cycling world wasn't ready to leave Lance behind. In August 2005, new rumors surfaced about Lance and drug use. In a French newspaper story, reporters claimed to have proof that Lance had used a performance-enhancing drug called EPO during the 1999 Tour.

Lance's response was the same as it had always been. He told reporters that he'd never used performance-enhancing drugs. He called the newspaper story a "witch hunt." The rumors angered Lance so much that he even talked about returning for the 2006 Tour de France, just to prove himself all over again.

Despite drug use rumors, it's doubtful that anything could ever hurt Lance Armstrong's legacy. He was a young, brash American in a sport dominated by Europeans. He was forgotten, beaten by cancer, and cast aside. But he never gave up on himself. Through sheer determination and will, he made himself into the greatest cyclist the world has ever known. It's possible that one day his record will be matched or broken, but his inspirational story—probably the greatest comeback story in sports history—will never be topped.

PERSONAL STATISTICS

Name:

Lance Edward Armstrong

Nickname:

Mellow Johnny

Born:

September 18, 1971

Height:

5'10"

Weight:

170 lbs.

Residence:

Austin, Texas

TOUR DE FRANCE STATISTICS (1999–2005)

Year	Team	Position	Time	Margin	2nd Place	Stages Won
1999	U.S. Postal	1	91:32:16	7:37	Zulle	4
2000	U.S. Postal	1	92:33:08	6:02	Ullrich	1
2001	U.S. Postal	1	86:17:28	6:44	Ullrich	4
2002	U.S. Postal	1	82:05:12	7:00	Beloki	4
2003	U.S. Postal	1	83:41:12	1:01	Ullrich	1
2004	U.S. Postal	1	83:36:02	6:19	Kloden	5
2005	Discovery Channel	1	86:15:02	4:40	Basso	1

Key: Margin: lead over the second-place finisher

GLOSSARY

cancer: a life-threatening disease in which some of the body's cells begin to grow out of control

chemotherapy: a cancer treatment in which powerful drugs are pumped directly into a patient's blood

criterium: a short bicycle race

doping: the use of illegal, performance-enhancing drugs

draft: to closely follow behind another racer to reduce wind resistance

peloton: the large pack of cyclists riding together during a race

sponsor: a company that pays an athlete or team in exchange for publicity

sprint: a short, flat ride that takes place at high speeds

steroid: an illegal drug that helps the body build muscle and endurance

time trial: a racing event in which each competitor starts alone and competes only against the clock

triathlon: a race that includes swimming, cycling, and running

tumor: a cancerous growth

BIBLIOGRAPHY

Armstrong, Kristin. *Lance Armstrong: The Race of His Life.* New York: Grosset & Dunlap, 2000.

Armstrong, Lance. *Every Second Counts.* With Sally Jenkins. New York: Broadway Books, 2003.

Armstrong, Lance. *It's Not About the Bike: My Journey Back to Life.* With Sally Jenkins. New York: Berkley Books, 2001.

Kelly, Linda Armstrong. *No Mountain High Enough: Raising Lance, Raising Me.* With Joni Rodgers. New York: Broadway Books, 2005.

Startt, James. *Tour de France, Tour de Force: A Visual History of the World's Greatest Bicycle Race.* San Francisco: Chronicle Books, 2003.

Stout, Glenn. *On the Bike with . . . Lance Armstrong.* Boston: Little, Brown, 2003.

Wilcockson, John. *23 Days in July: Inside Lance Armstrong's Record-Breaking Tour de France Victory.* Cambridge, MA: DaCapo Press, 2004.

WEB SITES

Lance Armstrong: The Official Site

http://www.lancearmstrong.com

Lance's official site includes news updates, a biography, fan club information, and links to his cancer foundation.

The Unofficial Lance Armstrong Fan Club

http://www.lancearmstrongfanclub.com

This fan site includes news updates, links to past stories about Lance, and a photo gallery.

Cyclingnews.com

http://www.cyclingnews.com

This site is the Internet center for cycling news, updates, and inside information.

Tour de France

http://www.letour.fr/indexus.html

The official site of the Tour de France includes detailed coverage of past Tours and previews of the next year's race.

INDEX